KY
KLÀ
DA

The Architect is Absent

Approaching the
Cycladic Holiday House

kyklàda.press

published by kyklàda.press
an imprint of PHOTOGRAPHIC
EXPANDED PUBLISHING ATHENS.

978-9-464202-82-3
D/2020/15058/03

@kyklada.press
www.kyklada.press

Constructing through Absence
Hülya Ertas

Most of the biographical texts on Iannis Xenakis start and advance with absence. The absence of his mother who died when he was five, the loss of an eye, the deprivation of his homeland Greece, the ending of his collaboration with Le Corbusier. His artistic virtuosity is depicted like a phoenix that keeps rising from these ashes of absence. But in the case of his only built project in Greece, Villa Mâche, it is Xenakis himself who is absent. He was not on site until after the completion of the project; he neither bodily experienced the slopes of the island in the development of his design nor led the construction process. Xenakis had to flee the country in 1947 following his political activities involving resistance with the National Liberation Front and Democratic Army of Greece (armed forces of Communist Party of Greece during the Greek Civil War). His initial death sentence turned into ten years imprisonment, and this verdict was in effect until the fall of the junta in 1974. This timeline is concur-

1

rent with the design and construction of the Villa Mâche. Designed in 1966 and realised between 1974 and 1977, its architect only saw the building after it was finished, during his trip to Greece in 1977.

Iannis Xenakis is not the first absentee architect on the site of a building, yet it is interesting to discover that the concept of the absentee designer is as old as the architecture profession itself. Even though the practice of building has been taking place for millennia the recognition of the architect's role is relatively new, dating back to the Renaissance. Leon Battista Alberti, one of the early architects of the Italian Renaissance, purposefully objected to the idea of architects being on site while their designs were being realised. In his view, "building should be left to the workers and their supervisors." (Carpo, 2011). In this way, Alberti distances himself from the building masters and claims his authorship as an architect. He, as the architect, should not direct the realisation of his ideas by commanding workers on site. Instead, he is a thinker that should be, and is, capable of communicating his ideas in written form or via models. This attitude, which today seems unacceptable to most practitioners, played a crucial role in the emergence of architecture as a profession.

Alberti's correspondence with the patron and building masters of Tempio Malatestiano demonstrates how he managed the process. During the construction of Tempio Malatestiano, Alberti sent drawings, a model, and various letters to

Rimini from Rome, where he was residing at the time. The correspondence was not only between Alberti and the master builders on the site, but also the master builders and the project's patron have corresponded regularly. Matteo de' Pasti, Pietro de' Gennari, Giovanni di maestro Alvise, Matteo Nutti wrote various letters to the patron Sigismondo Malatesta discussing the details of the construction. Among them, one is particularly interesting. It details Matteo de' Pasti suggesting to Sigismondo that he and Giovanni di maestro Alvise go to Rome to discuss the roof with Alberti (Tavernor, 1999). Later he adds that instead of him travelling to Rome, the master builder could be invited to have the discussion in Rimini. What is striking, though, is the recognition—made by all parties—of the absent architect at a time when the construction was typically centered around the local master builder who was active and present on the site. His absence implies "the transition from Brunelleschi's artisanal authorship (this building is mine because I made it) to Alberti's intellectual authorship (this building is mine because I designed it)." (Carpo, 2011).

Although Alberti's intentional absence derives from very different reasons, compared to Xenakis' semi-compulsory absence, we can see how the former paved the way for the latter by claiming the profession of architecture as a practice that is more than an act of building. During the construction of Villa Mâche, both the patron and the architect were residing in Paris, while the supervising architects were living in Greece and actively engaged on the site and in legal matters. Elisavet Kiourtsoglou's research shows that, in the case of Villa Mâche, the architect Iannis Xenakis initiated the process of finding local architects and then withdrew from the correspondence (Kiourtsoglou, 2019). The plan is first enclosed in a letter Iannis Xenakis wrote to his brother Cosmas, also an architect, asking for his help in finding the right local architect for the realisation of the house. Once the decision on the local partners is made, however, the correspondence takes place directly between the patron and local architects. It is Bernard-François Mâche who sends the plan enclosed in his letter to Popa Diamantopoulou in 1966, not Xenakis. Given their friendship and the fact that they lived in the same city, it is possible that Xenakis and Mâche discussed such issues in person. But there is little attention given to the design or how specific parts of the building might be realised. Contrary to correspondence between the master builders and the patron of Tempio Malatestiano, there is no discussion of how the building will be constructed. This discussion seems to take place only in a letter written in 1967 to Popa Diamantopoulou, in which Mâche proposes that one of the volumes be omitted and that they give up the external pavement due to cost. From this moment on, most of the correspondence is concerned with legal and economic issues and contains information about working

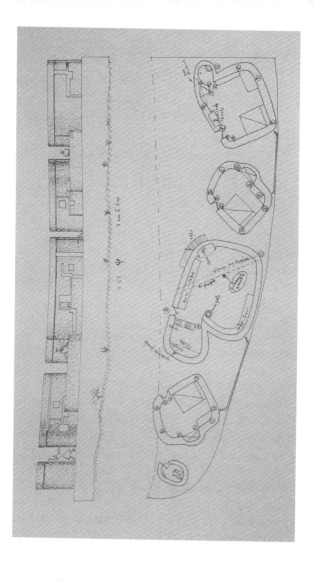

Fig. 1
North elevation and plan of Villa Mâche, Iannis Xenakis, 1966.

conditions on the construction site, the effect of the choice of artisans or the project's costs.

It is also important to note that, during the years of the Greek junta between 1967 and 1974, both the correspondence and the project were suspended (Kiourtsoglou, 2019). The restart of the project and the commencing of the construction are concurrent with the end of the military junta. The end of the regime was also significant in that it involved the removal of Xenakis' punishment and the revocation of him being prohibited from entering Greece. In 1974 Xenakis returned to Greece for a trip, but he did not go to Amorgos, where the construction site of Villa Mâche was ongoing. So the question remains: "why was Xenakis absent from his own work, of which large-sized photographs eventually ended up decorating his home in Paris?" (Kanach, 2008). Perhaps he had full confidence in the local architects Grigoris Diamantopoulos, Popa Diamantopoulou and Lia Bellou, and did not want to intervene in their work. But perhaps there are other, less material, clues to

Fig. 2
Tempio Malatestiano,
front façade, 2018.

6

the reasons for his absence.

The design and implementation of Villa Mâche coincided with a change in Xenakis' practice that derived from a change in the balance between his two main occupations: music and architecture. "From then on (after he quit his job at Le Corbusier's office), the 'architect-composer' was replaced by the 'composer-architect'. Gradually, Xenakis' ideas spread and his works began to be performed so that from 1965 onwards he was able to make a living from his music (through a combination of commissions and teaching). " (Sterken, 2004). From 1967 to 1987, Xenakis' architectural focus was mostly on *Polytopes*. These were spatial designs for enhancing the experience of sound and light and very much related to his understanding of music that takes its main inspiration from mathematics. Following Sterken's definition of Xenakis as the 'composer-architect', Xenakis' *Polytopes* are architectures for musical performances with an emphasis on music. One of his *Polytope* projects came into realisation after he visited the ancient site of Mycenae in November 1974. Welcomed like a national hero in his first return to his homeland, Xenakis did not visit the construction site of Villa Mâche and only saw "the site and neighboring villages for the first time in 1977, according to Mâche." (Kanach, 2008). During this first return trip to Greece, in the autumn of 1974, the construction was in full force with "6 workmen and 4 craftsmen", according to a letter sent by Lia Bellou to François-Bernard and Marie-

Luce Mâche on 27 September 1974 (Kiourtsoglou, 2019). Bellou also mentions harsh working conditions and the difficulties of getting materials and men on-site. This last piece of information, about the difficulties of transportation and access, provides crucial insight. Before jumping to conclusions about Xenakis' absence from the Villa Mâche construction site, it is helpful to consider the troubles people came across when traveling to Amorgos, this remote island in the Cyclades at that time.

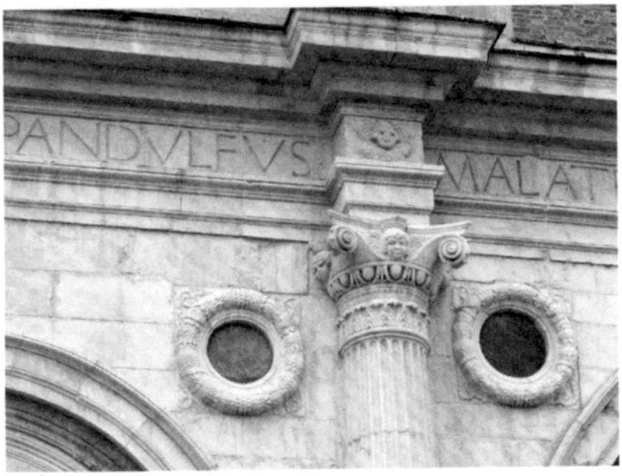
PANDVLFVS
MALAT

Both in the case of Villa Mâche and Tempio Malatestiano, the patrons are highly involved in the construction process. "But I trust in God that your Lordship will come to see this thing yourself before it is done and that you will decide what is best," wrote Pasti and Gennari in a letter to Sigismondo (Tavernor, 1999). There is a tone that reoccurs throughout these letters, which demonstrates the master builders' attempts at mediation between the project's architect and the patron. Their proposals, sometimes accompanied by new drawings,

Fig. 3
Tempio Malatestiano, detail of front façade, including Sigismondo Malatesta's signature, 2020.

are addressed to Sigismondo in order to assure him that the final result will be beautiful and in line with the initial design by Alberti, if not the same. In the correspondence about Villa Mâche, in contrast, there is little to no focus on the design. "You took the plans with you making it impossible for us to work. (...) Please send them back as soon as possible. We will make a copy and forward them to you. (...)" wrote Lia Bellou to François-Bernard and Marie-Luce Mâche (Kiourtsoglou, 2019). What this demonstrates is that the work on the site was based exclusively on Xenakis' design and that the local architects followed it strictly. Their sense of responsibility feels directed towards the designer-architect rather than the patron. The Tempio Malatestiano letters show master builders trying to please the patron Sigismondo, while Villa Mâche letters have a tone of local architects' motivation and desire to please the architect, Xenakis, by realising the project just as he drew it. Comparing two very different cases from very different time periods is not only difficult but somewhat problematic. The position of the architect as a professional has changed significantly, as have building technologies and social relations. Even so, comparing these two very different processes of realisation through the letters and drawings exchanged between the different parties involved in the projects remains not only interesting, but insightful.

"I have drawn a complex for him (free of charge, needless to say) that I would like to see

9

built if I were able to return to Greece" wrote Iannis Xenakis to his brother Cosmas in 1966 when he first told him of the project (Kiourtsoglou, 2019). Aside and on top of the conditions that forced Xenakis' distance from the project, it is possible that his absence was also, like Alberti's, an intention of the architect from the very beginning, borne out of a desire to see the project in its finished built state, but not before.

Hülya Ertas is an architect, editor, curator, and coordinator of exhibitions from Istanbul living in Brussels.

Carpo, Mario. The Alphabet and the Algorithm. Cambridge, USA: MIT Press, 2011.

Kiourtsoglou, Elisavet. Epistolary Architecture: When Writing Letters Created Modern Space, The Case of Iannis Xenakis' House at Amorgos, Greece. Text Journal, issue 55 (2019).

Sterken, Sven. Iannis Xenakis: Ingénieur et Architecte, PhD diss., Ghent University, 2004.

Kanach, Sharon. Music and Architecture by Iannis Xenakis. New York: Pendragon Press, 2008.

Tavernor, Robert. On Alberti and the Art of Building. New Haven: Yale University Press, 1999.

Meteorites
Mâkhi Xenakis

To write this short remembrance, perhaps it is best for me to be in Corsica, for my recollections here and show this very particular man in another light. He chose Corsica in 1951 to be the place where he would renew himself every summer, along with my mother and me. Corsica replaced Greece, where from 1947 to 1974 he was not permitted to travel because of his former political activities. In Corsica, he could calm his fears and shed his anxiety for a month, in a hand-to-hand confrontation with the wildest aspects of nature that he could find.

As I write these lines, I have close by me one of his many small notebooks, where he jotted down with his finest pen an idiosyncratic juxtaposition of notes, mathematical equations, sketches and Greek letters. September 1951: "How to introduce voices, cries of pain, sobs, into music?" September 1952: "I must continue to strip down sound and rhythm. To reduce them to their most primitive expression... To find composition in its secret hiding place at the deepest level of primitive art. The opposite of modern diversity and complexity! The origin of music, that's what must be put back into place... Relearning to touch sound with our hands—that's the heart, the essence of music!"

The more I speak about him with my mother these days, the more we become convinced that although during the rest of the year my father showed every evidence of a very erudite and rational mind, linking music, architecture and mathematics, the main motor of his acts was a deep wound, profound suffering that grew familiar to us and whose traces we find in most of his music. This suffering certainly stemmed from the tragedies he lived through during the Civil War in Greece, but also from his childhood. When he was five, his mother, in the course of giving birth to a baby girl, died. Brutally deprived of his family cocoon, he was obliged to construct himself alone.

I believe that he struggled to exercise this stunning shock of death, through his music and during every instant of his life. One of the things he said to me most often was "Mâ, do you realize that we're météorites; almost as soon as we're born, we have to disappear?" This enthusiasm, this permanent quest for the primitive force in art, takes me back again to images of him in Corsica.

Sitting cross-legged, he would pour over a book of Plato or mathematics. He sometimes stared at the sky, searching for that particular moment when he could at last, in extreme, hand-to-hand combat, draw close to the untamed elements of nature, to nourish and renew himself in them.

He's standing now, facing the raging sea, his face radiant, peaceful at last, reflecting a particular serenity that signifies that this moment won't escape him any longer.

We'll be able to go out in the kayak now. The gigantic waves break over us with a terrifying roar; we are completely immersed in their white spray. We can't breathe. Everything is white, deafening. And again, I hear his voice, barely audible among the sounds that have become suddenly deafening, upright, upright, upright!!!! And the movement of our oars accelerates, to maintain the boat against the waves, or we will capsize and may be shattered against the rocks...

The thunder rumbles, we've taken refuge in our tent. And again his face is radiant, peaceful. He uses his watch to calculate meticulously the number of seconds between the brutal bursts of lightning that tear apart the night and the explosions of thunder as they grow closer and closer to us. When the storm is at last directly above our heads, he leaves the tent, half-naked, he runs and disappears little by little into this grandiose spectacle of sound and apocalyptic light.

In the early morning, when dew covers every particle of the arid countryside, he crouches for hours, scrutinizing each very particular spiderweb. A multitude of parallel stretched lines sketch out complex architectures comprising cut-off cones, convex and concave surfaces conjoined. They are the natural ancestors of the *Philips Pavilion* and the *Polytopes*…

So many other memories surge forth now, and each of them takes me to these overwhelming, founding moments, this man who was my father, and the violence and the special force that I find in his music today.

Corsica, August 2009.

Mâkhi Xenakis is a visual artist living in Paris and daughter of Iannis Xenakis.

Originally published in the catalogue of The Drawing Center for the exhibition: Iannis Xenakis, composer, architect, visionary. New York: 2010.

Summer Home for François-Bernard Mâche, by Iannis Xenakis, 1966–74
Sharon Kanach

During the summer of 1965, the French composer, Hellenist and close friend of Xenakis, François-Bernard Mâche, bought a small piece of property on an island in the Cyclades. The site is rather isolated and was accessible only by boat and then by foot at the time and had neither running water nor electricity. (Now, there is solar energy and a freshwater spring was found on-site and access to the site has recently been paved)[1]. In 1966, Mâche asked Xenakis to design a summer home for his family there. Since at that time Xenakis was still banned from Greece, he had to study the terrain from photographs brought back to Paris by Mâche.

Originally, Xenakis designed four separate units or cells, according to the wishes of the family who wanted to maintain independent spaces. Finally, due to costs and the symmetry of two identical volumes, the final project comprised only three units —a master suite with an independent full bath, a communal area with the kitchen and living space with a fireplace, and finally, a guest area with a small bath.

Fig. 4

Construction began only in 1974 and was accomplished by local craftsmen who, because of distance and heat, began work every day at around 5:00 AM. Building supplies arrived by boat and were transported up the approximately 70 meter (approximately 230 ft) slope by donkeys.

In his plans, Xenakis was most concerned with creating a general form for the ensemble that would harmonize with the natural contour of the underlying bay as well as the actual terrain that had been terraced many, many years earlier for agricultural purposes.

Because of this terracing, some of the foundations for part of the house are actually as deep as the height of the finished structure. Simply excavating the construction's foundation took three weeks.

The organic, rounded forms seem clearly inspired by local (Cycladic) architecture, in which village walls are often curved, following the contours of the landscape. Many of the furnishings are

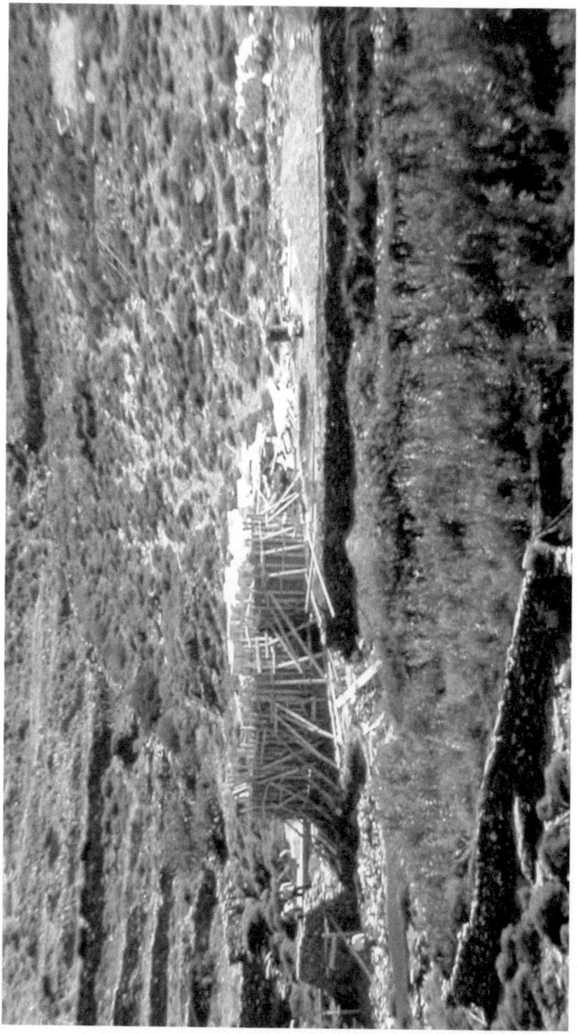

Fig. 4
Villa Mâche, construction site, building supplies arrive by boat.
Fig. 5
Villa Mâche, construction site, formwork.

built into the structure, also a local practice. However, Xenakis was surprised by these similarities when visiting the site and neighboring villages for the first time in 1977, according to Mâche.

The window openings, for the most part fixed, and cast directly into the supporting walls by pouring concrete into molds, appear to come from the same neume-based inspiration as the roof kindergarten in Nantes and the terrace wall at La Tourette designed by Xenakis during his Le Corbusier years. Nonetheless, Mâche affirms that this is a result of Xenakis's play on his initials, mainly the letter 'F'. In addition to their aesthetic appeal and functional lighting, these openings were placed in order to frame specific perspectives.

Another remarkable feature of this construction is the 40 centimeter (approximately 15 in) wide *path of light*, (Fig. 23) that Xenakis designed, splitting the living room's ceiling: an ultimate evolution of the *light machine guns* and *light cannons* from La Tourette. According to Bernard-François Mâche, the sunlight is so intense there in the summer, that it is necessary to screen this opening. True to his passion for new natural light sources, all three cells plus the small independent bathroom have raised ceilings that are 'detached' from the intersections of the supporting walls.

Xenakis here accomplishes yet one more architectural feat: creating openings for indirect zenith light.

Xenakis always considered this realization

an integral part of his oeuvre. In his home in Paris, several enlarged photos of this summer home adorn corridor walls. In a book on computers and their visual environments, Xenakis chose a photo of this house (among other elements) to represent his work.

Fig. 6
Villa Mâche as seen from the path connecting the street to the sea, 2018.

Sharon Kanach is an American musician who has been living in France since being a university student. Her research, although primarily archival based, aims to foster prospective creative developments.

1. This last detail about the newly paved road was confirmed to the author by e-mail on Oct. 22, 2020 by David Bergé.

Originally published in: Xenakis, Iannis, and Kanach, Sharon. Music and Architecture: Architectural Projects, Texts, and Realizations. Hillsdale, New York: Pendragon Press, 2008.

Fig. 7,8
Villa Mâche as seen from the sea, 2018.

Fig. 8

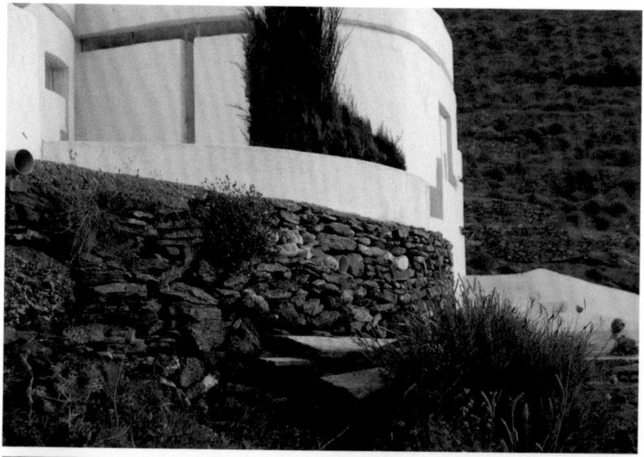

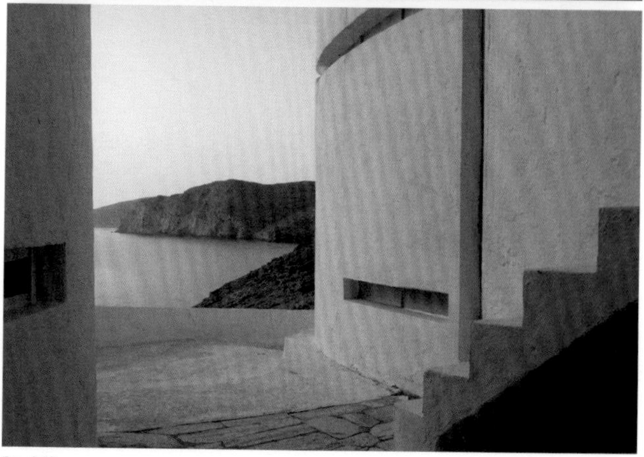

Fig. 9,10

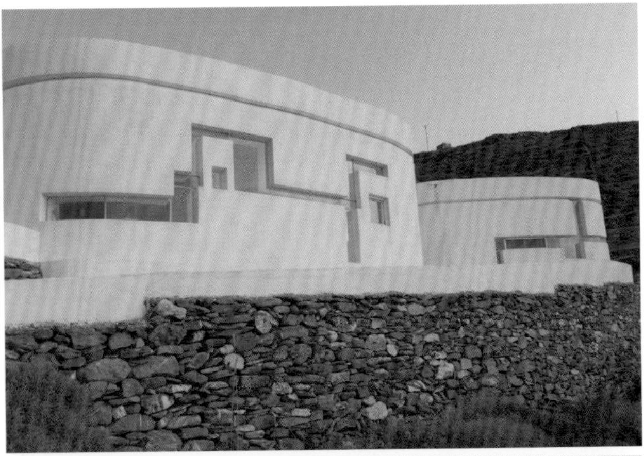

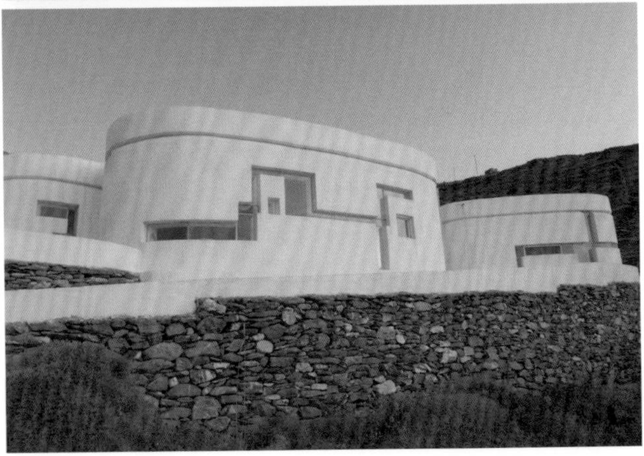

Fig. 11,12

Fig. 13

Fig. 15

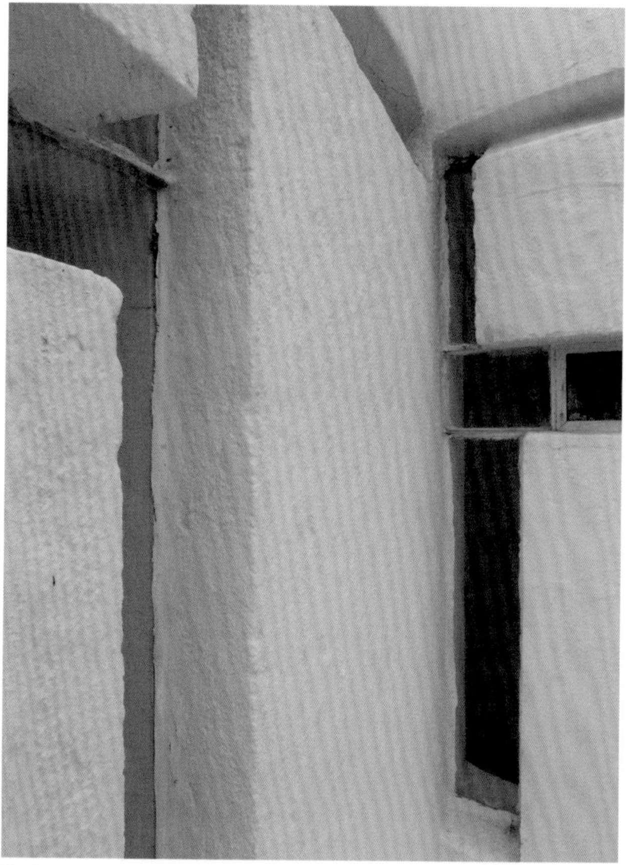

Fig. 16

Fig. 17

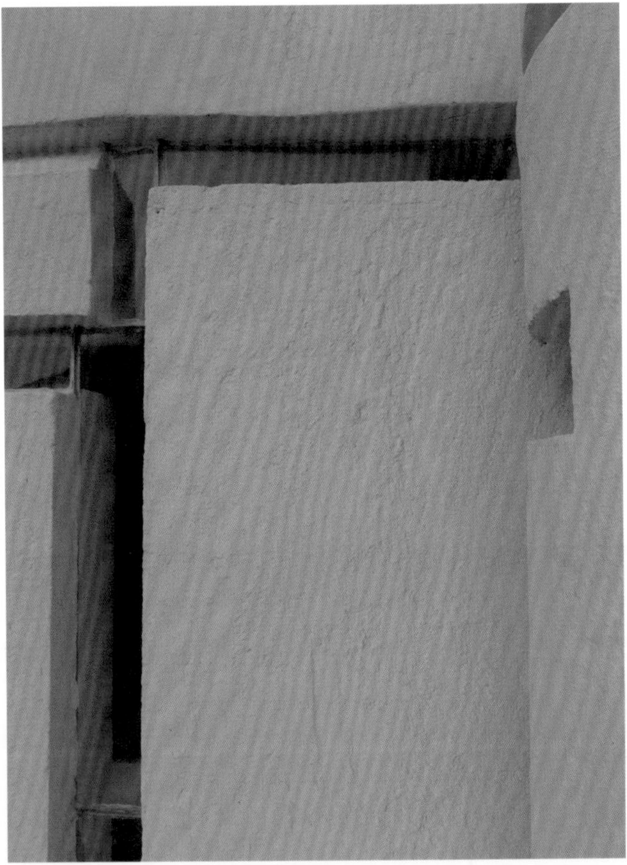

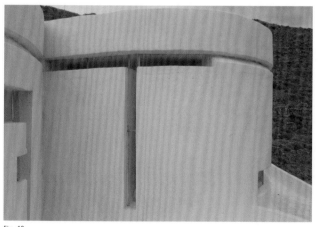

Fig. 18

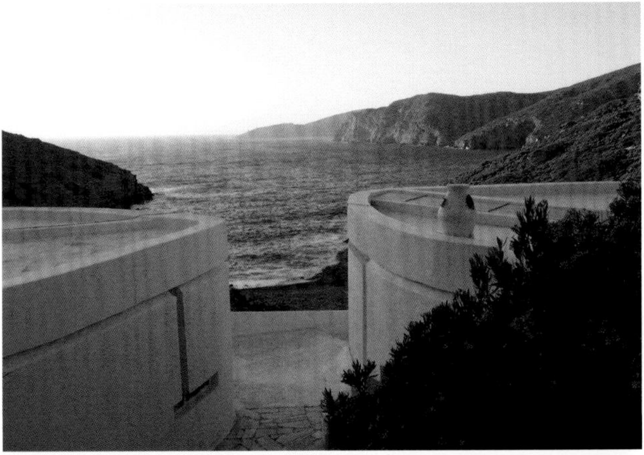

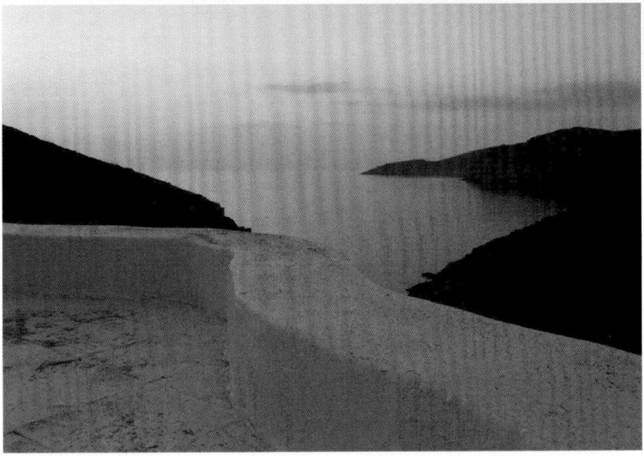

Fig. 19, 20

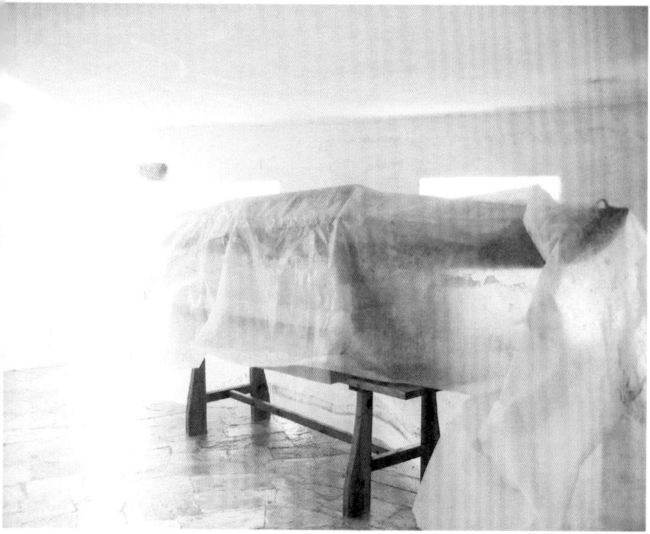

Fig. 21

Fig. 9–20, 25
Villa Mâche, exterior, 2020.

Fig. 21–24
Villa Mâche, interior, 2005.

Fig. 22

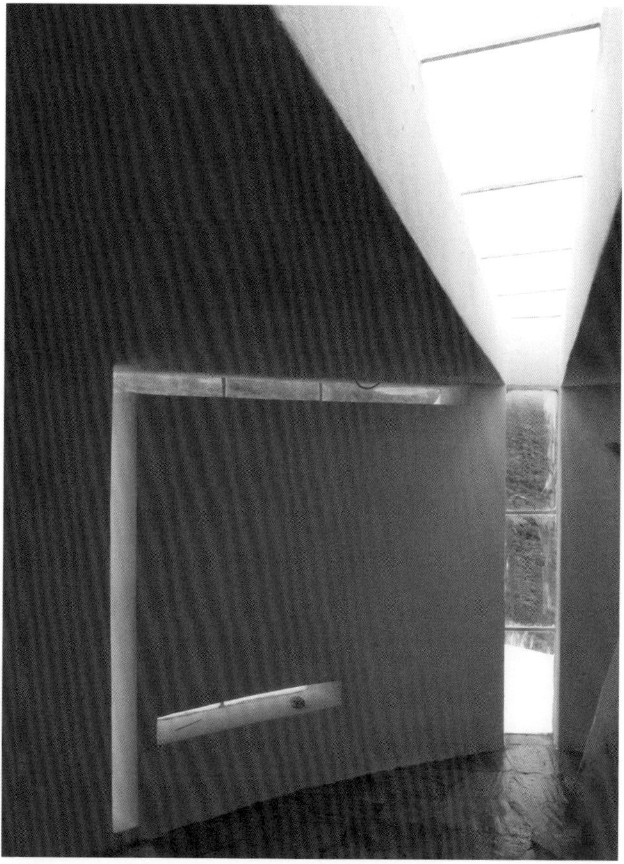

Fig. 23

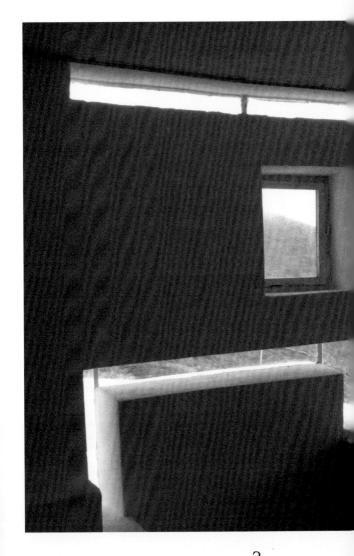

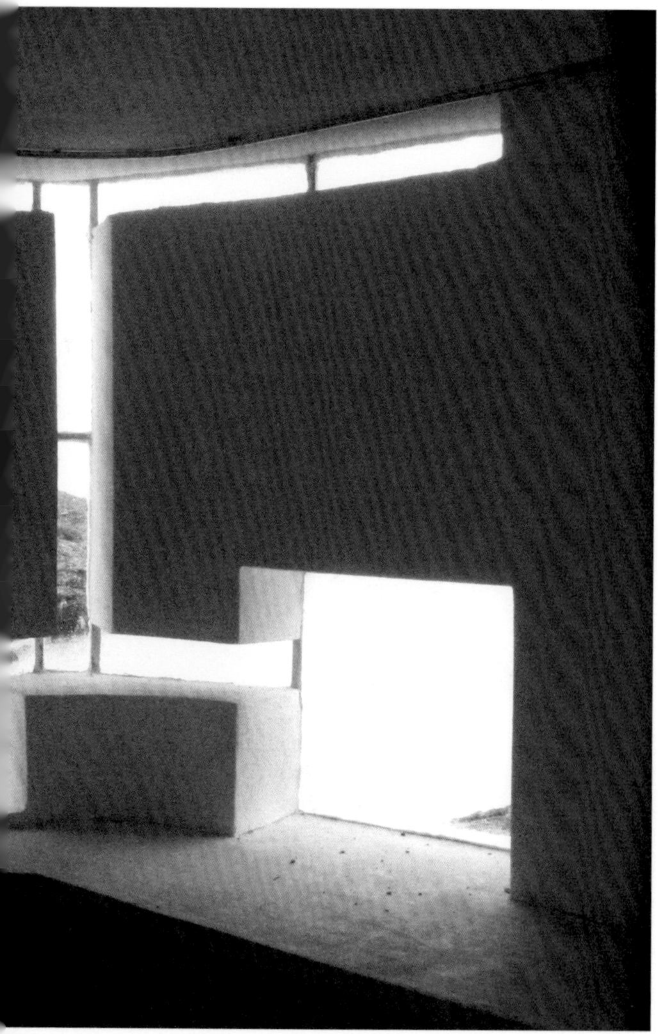

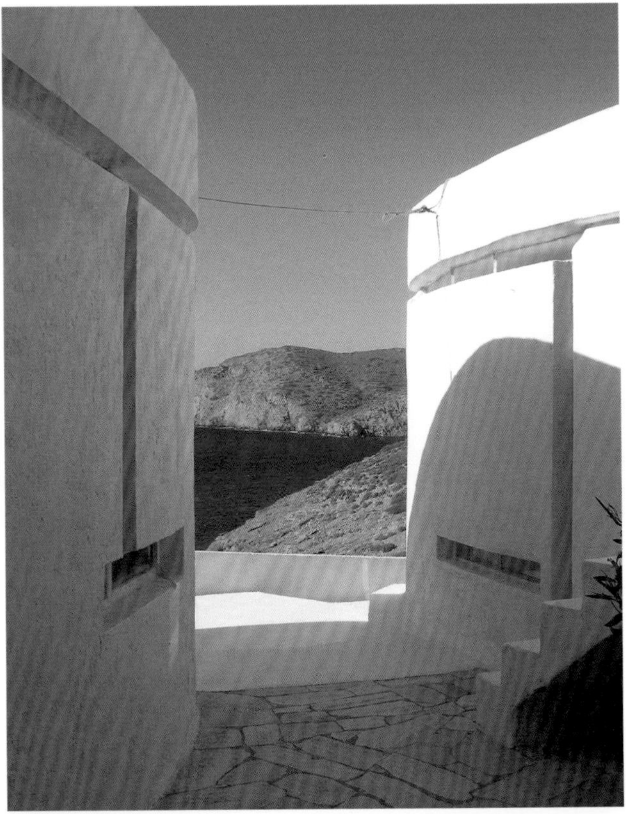

Fig. 25

Villa Mâche: a harsh hijack against the space of the sun
David Bergé

what
at first sight
looks like
a nice twist on the white Cycladic house,
in which
square out-lines were changed into curved ones;
in which
the vacationers' mind
can lose itself temporarily
staring at
and falling asleep with
the noise of the present
—the sound of the sea.

what
at first sight
looks like
a place in which
the vacationer finds shelter
from the wind and sun,
is here

4
1

a harsh hijack against the space of the sun:
fissures. wounds knifed into whitened concrete
an arrow slit, a loophole, une meurtrière
bunker windows
from which to shoot the enemy
—the outside:
light,
noise,
other people.

> the exigency to cut all views against
> the destructive light out there
>
> an argument between the focus inside
> and the other out there
>
> an architecture activating its user
> not comforting her
>
> an architecture imploring the entire
> body to move
>
> an architecture commissioned to
> monastically write music inside.

outside
five scattered houses
inside
curves changing into squares
according to need and function
cupboard, kitchen, bench.

five monastic cells to
write music,
sleep,
cook,
read,
shit.

David Bergé is an artist living in Athens and Brussels. He works with site-specific interventions, installations, Walk Pieces, and book projects.

Traveling to the Cyclades: Modernist Projections
Dimitra Kondylatou

The formation of the Modern Traveler

For many centuries travel has been an aspect of people's work, leisure and cultural formation. In a sense, travel makes the world go round, as people move for political, financial, medical, professional, or cultural reasons; in search of safety, opportunities, novelty, or love. They travel out of necessity, out of curiosity, out of the ordinary. In this text I trace the extraordinariness of travel to the Cyclades from the late 19th to the late 20th century. I do so through an examination of the mythologies, belonging to different chronologies and disciplines, that have generated the most solid and recurrent representations of Greece: the ancient past; the white houses of the Aegean; nature, landscapes, and beaches.

Before the turn of the 20th century, the poetics and politics of modern travel were shaped —to a great extent—by its most prominent practitioners: the white, male, and affluent members of the industrially advanced societies of imperial powers, principally England, later France and Germany, among others. Occupying a visible place in the public sphere, they were provided with the time, space, and authority to write and publish their observations and perceptions, as well as their admiration for and disappointment in the places they came to inspect, explore, or venerate. Their letters, diaries, memoirs, and books offer insights, not only into traveling habits of the authors, but also into their subjectivties, temperaments, and influences. Forming an essential school in travel literature, these texts bequeathed knowledge to future travelers, and influenced their expectations, feelings, and behavior.

After the constitution of the Greek state in 1830, signifying a decisive orientation towards Europe, Greece became a more common destination for travel writers of the time. In their texts, time and space intermingle to present the ancient Greek past as an idyllic, familiar topos: a timeless land holding an ecumenic heritage of which they were the spiritual shareholders—the origins of Western civilization. Their visions and opinions were influenced by the literature written by their predecessors. And it was with these texts that travel writers of the early 19th century conversed more than with those who met in these travels, whom sometimes they confronted as figures emerging straight from ancient myths. All their points of reference and identification were situated in the past. Cultural travelers of that time visited mainland Greece, and the most important ancient sites in Athens, Delphi, the Peloponnese, and a few islands. At the same time, the strategic location and growing importance of the Aegean islands as maritime transit stations attracted many researchers who were on medical, diplomatic, commercial, and archaeological missions. Their texts reveal important details on everyday life in these societies, while retaining a tone of superiority towards them.

Near the end of the 19th century, the widespread use of the steam engine arranged space in a different way. Routes and infrastructure initially established for maritime trade and war could be used for other kinds of journeys. Several individual initiatives, such as Thomas Cook's first organized excursion in 1841 and his company's subsequent activity, had already set the basis for tourism. The ability to travel faster and easier was constantly growing and larger populations discovered the pleasures of travel and holidays, usually in the countryside of the modern metropolises they were residing. During the interbellum, however, international cultural travel was still a privilege of the upper classes. Better prepared and more socially aware than their predecessors, 20th century travelers interacted more with the people and the landscapes they encountered. Yet they remained mesmerized by the ancient ruins. In this way, their texts contributed to the tradition of travel literature established in previous centuries.

Letters from the 'Land of the Moon'

"Why not live like this forever?" wrote Virginia Woolf in her diary on Sunday 24th of April, 1932, during her second trip to Greece. The way she experienced life in Greece in the interwar period was free and wild, filled with thyme and cypress. Woolf's sensitive observations and descriptions of her visits to ancient ruins, encounters with local people, and walks in the countryside are filled with ambivalence and wonder. Despite her insightful approach to the place that differentiated her from her—most frequently male—predecessors, she remained to a great extent under the romanticizing spell of the literary tradition they had established. On 2nd of May, in a letter to her sister, Vanessa Bell, Woolf wrote that Greece is with no doubt the most beautiful country left untouched. Further, Woolf marks Greece 'an uncivilized country'. The ambiguity of the word 'uncivilized' describes the coarseness—in the absence of modernity—of a rural life shaped within financial austerity in a land, long-contested between the East and the West. Woolf's choice of this word also highlights a contrast with England, where the country's international financial, colonial, and military dominance, social and religious transformations, and technological advancements that reached almost all English regions, cultivated a feeling that life was fast-paced and in constant progress. Similar developments were taking place in Greece's larger cities, yet on a much smaller scale; while the countryside remained organized around a primary sector economy. Woolf described Greek people as subjects of the vast distances of the landscape, unable to tame its old, wild, stony, and rough character. Notes from Woolf's diary entries on the same day also elaborate a vision of the landscape as the land of the moon. Comparing it to English landscapes, Woolf speaks of a lack in the Greek landscape of any traces or signs of the previous centuries. This quality—the absence of layers, buildings, or infrastructure—leads Woolf to the observation that the landscape appears as though it could belong to 300 BC, a date that 'occupied Greece' and still holds it under a 'dead sun'. Woolf, like most of her contemporaries, seems to have been carried away by traditional, even stereotypical, romantic interpretations. What was perceived as a chronological gap with regards to Western progress was a period of regional transformation that later saw the erasure of some traces of the Ottoman Empire and the construction of the new Greek state. From this perspective, traveling to Greece seemed like time travel. Woolf, like many other European travelers of the time, was perceiving a gap, which instead of dividing, it bridged the ancient past with modern Greece—that in their eyes did not appear very modern. Yet, in contrast to the previous generation of travelers, it seduced them. Right before leaving Greece, on the 8th of May, Woolf expressed a desire that went unfulfilled: to return every year, live in a tent, and eat nothing but bread, butter, and eggs. She could then get rid of the burden of the English decency, conventionality, fame and wealth, and become a real lover of life. Arguably, this marked a new step in travel culture: to travel out of nostalgia for, and in pursuit of, a 'pre-modern' life, a life that one may have never experienced before, or may not have experienced for a while. Certainly, though, it was in pursuit of a life one had heard or read of.

Weaving Myths on Board

The year after Woolf's trip to Greece, the fourth *Congrès Internationaux d'Architecture Moderne* (CIAM, International Congress of Modern Architecture), under the title *The Functional City*, took place from 29th July to 31st August 1933 on board the *Patris* II ship that departed on a return trip from Marseille to Piraeus. The international architects and artists on board had the chance to visit the Greek antiquities in Athens and some surrounding islands such as Aegina, Serifos, Ios, and Santorini. The stone-built houses and villages on the islands seemed to embody an intergenerational popular knowledge of Greece. They were shaped by local idioms and traditions, and domestic maritime exchanges of building materials, technologies, and methods. In the eyes of the international architectural elite, the anonymous Cycladic architecture bore the basic elements of Modernist architecture: simplicity, functionality, and scale.

Modernism was consolidated during the historical period between the two World Wars through national, artistic and ideological conflicts, and constructions that caused significant social transformations. The avant-garde movements, opposing the old academies, made radical proposals for new forms of art, architecture, and urban planning. However, their opposition to the classicist tradition and the academy was claimed with such force that new traditions were created. Modernist concepts of innovation and universalism often included cultural appropriation, and their ideological claims were usually put forth by a 'genius man', and intermingled with personal ambitions. The remnants and pasts of other cultures were essential components of the Modernist consciousness and were used by the pioneers in art and architecture, in their search for truth and universality, to solidify and legitimate their ideas. In this sense, the fourth CIAM acquired a symbolic significance through its palindromic movement between industrial Marseille and classical Athens, considered to be the cradle of civilization and the origin of the *polis*. Within this transit, the vernacular Cycladic house acquired its special symbolic position among other, similar settlements in the wider Mediterranean region due to its location on the land where the Cycladic civilization had bloomed centuries ago. The particular characteristics and forms of Cycladic sculpture and architecture, dissolving in the light of the Greek landscape, were perceived as archetypal and acquired a metaphysical aura.

The 'myth of the Aegean', being in part an ideological construction of Modernism, resonated differently to the various actors involved according to their cultural and political interests. The square lime-washed box epitomized this symbolic transition from the Antiquity to Modernism. Rather than being regarded as a reference point that would generate new formations, it was substantialized as a confirmation of Modernism's claims and ambitions. Greek artists and architects of the same generation claimed a part of this new value deriving from the Aegean, and capitalized on the Cycladic house and landscape to intensify their dialogue with the European avant-gardes. In their own search for innovation and 'truth', they attributed an ultimate value to art and added the element of 'Greekness' to Modernist principles. This element of 'Greekness' was an ideological construction, of national spirit, that sought to unite the ancient Greek past, the Byzantine period and the nature and culture of the Aegean. But this effort relied on the exclusion of any other cultural elements that did not fit with the desired representation or message. Through these contrived aesthetic affinities these artists and architects claimed a spiritual and even genetic descent from the ancient populations who were residing in the same geographical area centuries ago, and in doing so, disregarded its diversity and multiculturality.

This attempt to bridge the chronological and cultural distance between modern and ancient forms, through the instrumentalisation of nature and popular culture, seems to be a paradoxical and complex project considering the centrality of the industrial revolution and the rise of the machine to Modernism. The teleological approach to ancient culture and primal forms suggests a different understanding of history. Or, rather, its substitution for myths and symbols that tended to idealize the past to fit the future and vice versa. Through this narrative that represented Greece as a timeless, ecumenical, archetypal land of culture, art and spirit, the Modernists tended to 'civilize' the rural Greek landscape by imposing on it their gaze. At the same time, they attributed a civilizing character to it, derived from this transhistorical and transcultural construction.

Fig. 26
Villa Mâche, patio, 2018.

"For moderns, reality and authenticity are thought to be elsewhere: in other historical periods and other cultures, in purer, simpler lifestyles. In other words, the concern of moderns for 'naturalness', their nostalgia and their search for authenticity are not merely casual and somewhat decadent, though harmless, attachments to the souvenirs of destroyed cultures and dead epochs. They are also components of their conquering spirit of modernity—the grounds of its unifying consciousness. (...) Every nicely motivated effort to preserve nature, primitives and the past, and to represent them authentically, contributes to an opposite tendency—the present is made more unified against its past, more

Fig. 27
Tourism infrastructures,
Serifos, 2016.

in control of nature, less a product of history. (...) But unique to the modern world is its capacity to transform material relations into symbolic expressions and back again, while continuing to differentiate or multiply structures." (MacCannell, 1996, p.3)

The paradoxical relationship of Modernism with the 'pre-modern' in the Aegean can be traced through another ideological device: white color. In L'Art Décoratif d'Aujourd'hui (The Decorative Art of Today), Le Corbusier, in defence of simplicity, argued that civilizations who did not use external decorations were superior to those who did. In the essay, Le Corbusier notes the following observation: "during my trips, I found white lime-wash everywhere where the 20th century had not yet arrived." In fact, most houses on the Cycladic islands were made of stone and clay and retained their stone walls unpainted, or were painted in colors found in nature and made from oxidised iron and other natural resources: ochre, red, indigo and grey. The bare stone and the natural colors camouflaged the settlements against the frequent pirate attacks in the 18th century. On the contrary, limewash was an expensive material and mostly used for aesthetic and practical reasons in rich houses and mansions located in the islands' capitals, Choras. As well as being an indication of wealth, lime wash and marble dust were used for extra stability and sustainability against humidity. In less expensive

houses and households, since the rule of Capo-
distrias in the 1830s, limewash was used for sanitary reasons as a disinfectant, on the occasion of
pandemic outbreaks, and was applied perimetrically around streets and settlements and house
entrances. Occasionally, there were decrees for
total sanitary white-washing. It is said that during
the dictatorship of Ioannis Metaxas, a piece of 1938
legislation obliged all islanders to white-wash their
houses due to an outbreak of cholera. At the time
of the first visits of European Modernists to the
Cyclades, there were lime-washed houses—sometimes whole villages consisting of them—sporadi-
cally located among multicolored houses. Despite
this, the focus of the travelers was placed on white.
The motif of the white house standing out amongst
the wilderness and bathed in light is a predominant
feature in most modern artistic representations of
the Cyclades.

White is achromatic; it is not actually a
color, but reflects and scatters all visible wave-
lengths of light. On an aesthetic level, the white
color enhances the structure of the house against
the landscape and makes visible the volumes and
plasticity of the settlements. On a symbolic level,
inspired by Neoplatonic thought, it functions as an
archetypal mold: that which is timeless, spiritual,
abstract, clean and pure. It evokes the whiteness of
ancient marbles—the symbolic foundations of the
white Western civilization—in their ruinous state,
even though in their functional state ancient mar-

bles were decorated in colors similar to those used on the exteriors of the Aegean houses. In this sense, white, except for the light, reflects some aspects of the 'Greek narrative': an uninterrupted linear history linking the Antiquity to Modernity, symbolized by the Cycladic architecture and light.

The Modern Traveler after World War II

The Universal Declaration of Human Rights, adopted by the United Nations in 1948 after World War II, proclaimed the right of every person to paid holidays —turning travel from privilege to personal right. The democratization of leisure suggested that all social relations in modern societies were organized around work. The division of the 24-hour day into eight hours of work, eight hours of free time and eight hours of sleep, normalized this structuring of everyday life. While work and sleep were fixed, the intermediary zone of leisure was organized by the state and subsequently shaped by the individual, while the market would later penetrate it. The paradigm of early noble travelers, for whom the encounter with other cultures and natural landscapes was a means for their spiritual and cultural formation, set the basis for the organization of leisure in modern societies. The planning of specific spaces that provided contact with nature, the ability to rest, and informative activities, was first implemented in modern designs for functional cities with the construction of parks, leisure areas, and programs. This soon spread to other places as the intense rhythm of labor and urbanization in Western European cities cultivated a need to escape.

The rise of tourism promised the fulfilment of the individuals' desires and fantasies for another kind of life, away from work and out of the ordinary. This desire was for a life organized on peaceful—after the long wars—lands and fields of leisure and pleasure. The fast-developing financial sector fed the collective imagination with representations of non-industrialized societies. Such visions were romanticized by earlier travelers, but were now being produced and consumed on a massive scale with the mediation of national policies and private investments. Commercialized tourism representations subsumed travel literature. Except for travel guides that had been published since the beginning of the 19th century, travel literature had been sparser and more individual in character until this point. Now, it was enriched by picturesque and stereotypical cinematic representations that aestheticized places and peoples, and exoticized their hard earned lives.

The new generation of travelers, following massively addressed guidelines and infrastructure, wandered in structured systems of symbols, signs and significations—seeking their confirmation. Their voyeuristic gaze projected upon other peoples' habits concealed their own repulsed desires and obscure fantasies. In their search for happiness and freedom, they got only a latent impression of this place or that aspect of life. The eyes of their traveling companions reflected the life they wanted to escape. They thus became desperately nostalgic for a life they perceived as unique and more real, but this nostalgia was not accompanied by any real intention to pursue such a life.

Tourist Consumption of Islands and Myths

On a geopolitical level, tourism became a tool for cultural diplomacy. It mediated differences between nation states and was a lever for the financial recovery of 'less-developed' places, who were now able to dynamically rejoin the geopolitical map. Favored by a mild climate, stunning nature and mythical history, the Mediterranean seaside and countryside —and its islands, more precisely—were of the first regions that became tourist destinations. The insularity of the island—stereotypically conceived as utopic—became a counterexample to the suffocating and centrally organized life of the city. The existence of small infrastructures for maritime and aerial transportation, remnants from the war, made the islands accessible and was a crucial factor in their massive appeal. The new tourist destinations could be reached beside the regular ferry routes, by private boats and charter flights. The governors and citizens of Mediterranean countries, exhausted and impoverished by the wars, realized tourism's power to summon its customers to the source. They readily joined this peculiar industry that exports its commodities where it produces them.

After the end of the Civil War in 1949 and the country's participation in the Marshall Plan from 1947 to 1951, tourism gradually became one of the fundamental sectors of the Greek economy —which continued to be in a recovery process. The architecture of this time expressed the social transformations taking place in the country. Initiated by the *Greek National Tourism Organization* (GNTO) in the 1950s, Xenia network—one of the biggest state-run hospitality infrastructure projects in the country —set the basis for architectural experimentation with spatial and aesthetic Modernist forms in dialogue with the natural and historical surroundings. Alongside this were growing private investments and a central administration planning the tourism development in coordination with local authorities.

With the arrival of tourism, the Cycladic islands—drained of their population due to urban-

Fig. 28
Xenia Hotel, Mykonos,
architect: Aris Konstantinidis, 1983.

ization, migration and poverty — turned their economies from the first to third sector. Their inhabitants abandoned their agricultural activities to provide services for the new, temporary residents who longed for the sensation of their holiday. The Aegean islands, once depicted as wild and mystical places, became mythical sites for collective pleasure and sightseeing. Time began to be perceived differently, as the construction of asphalt roads that served tourist mobility carved the slopes and the mountains, and the proliferating vehicles eliminated the distances that had seemed enormous to previous travelers. In the deriving tourist narratives, the elements extracted from the natural, historical and cultural contexts were mixed with modern and modernized things and people. Culture, nature and everyday local life were turned into commodities, sold and consumed in the form of spectacles, attractions, and experiences. Thus, the myth of Greece and its narratives—shaped by the idealizing formulations of the Greek and European Modernists and conceptually enfolded in the construction of a unifying national narrative—was incorporated into the country's tourism branding.

There is a rumor about Queen Frederica of Greece showing the Prime Minister, Konstantinos Karamanlis, in 1955, a picture of some white, well-preserved houses in Mykonos with the suggestion that they could be used for the promotion of tourism in the Aegean. The growing popularity of the white Cycladic house and its recurrent repre-

6
1

sentation in tourism slowed down architectural experimentation on the Cycladic islands. Debates within Greek architectural circles were initiated during the development of island tourism, and raised concerns over the construction scale and the buildings' typologies. Until the middle part of the 20th century, there was little divergence in the suggested forms, except for some older—public and religious —buildings that followed the continental paradigm.

Shades of White

The discordance of interests of visitors, residents, artists, architects, and the state created a vicious circle, a mise en abyme that proliferated the whiteness of the Cycladic settlements. Islanders, understanding the deriving symbolic value of this situation and speculating on its financial potential, participated in the lime-washing of houses and villages. This took place as a result of both personal initiative and national policy.

One of the most decisive moments was the obligatory whitening ordered by the military junta in 1972. According to the decree, "among other restrictions on construction, it is forbidden to apply many hues on the house façades, and it has been decided that the dominating color of houses should be white (...) which is a particular characteristic of the Cyclades islands and generally a subconscious duty of all inhabitants (...) to achieve full uniform-

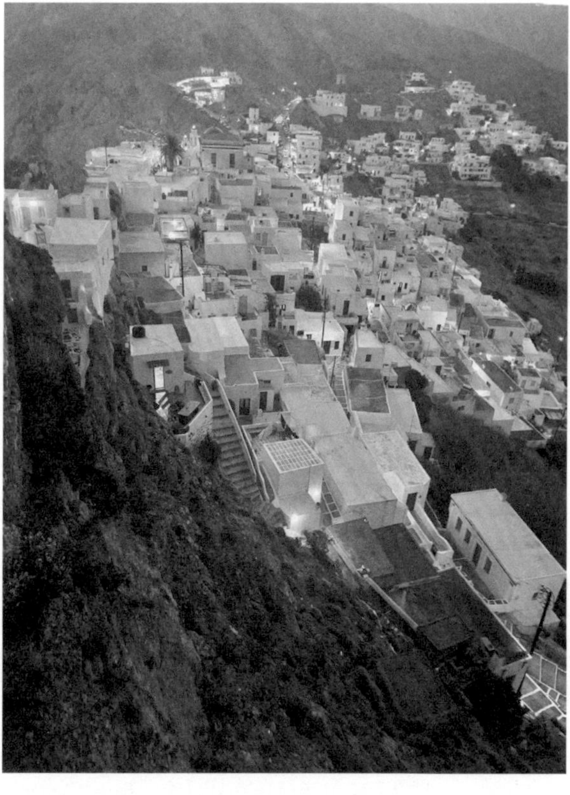

Fig. 29
Serifos, Chora, 2020.

ity in harmony with the peculiar color of Cyclades islands". White was instrumentalized to serve the totalitarian ideology of homogeneity, expressed by white houses with blue doors and windows. On one hand, this was a reference to the colors of the Greek flag, resonating nationalist feelings and symbolizing the Greek nature—blue for the sea and white for the seafoam. On the other hand, this was part of the construction of a national brand according to the regime's aesthetics and used for tourism purposes. The military junta's extreme liberal financial policy focused on the intensification of tourist activity through measures that facilitated the building of infrastructure, big-scale hotels and tourist accommodations scattered across Greece. Construction accelerated, assisted by previous legislation such as a 1928 regulation that allowed the construction of countryside buildings in plots larger than one acre located outside of villages and settlements (although this was partly restricted following the 1978 legislation on traditional settlements). In the Cyclades, white villas and hotels retaining the exterior form of the Cycladic house, were built in concrete instead of stone, and painted white. They gradually spread on various spots outside the islands' settlements looking like decontextualized white dots scattered around the landscape. The junta's 1972 decree presented whiteness, already existing in the architecture of the region, as a Cycladic trait to be preserved for a long time. Indeed, in the 2003 legislation concerning traditional construction on the island of Amorgos, it is mentioned that houses' exteriors should either be lime-washed or painted with white color, according to the architectural standards of the region.

The Modernist exaltation of the white vernacular house dissolved in its tourism representations. The tourist request for assimilation into local, 'authentic' life, was architecturally translated as an urge for the reproduction of the 'traditional' white houses. The metaphysical property of the Cycladic house was transmitted from the 'archetypal' to the 'traditional'. Critics of white-washing argued that this dry reproduction lacked any inspiration, thought, and innovation, stripped the Cycladic house of its primal character and treated architecture as scenography, serving the tourism branding of the region and transforming the islands into theme parks. They added to this that the whitening of the settlements affected the scale of the landscape. The optical illusion of natural unity, once caused by the stone houses being hidden amidst the stones, was ruined by the white volumes that stood distinct from the surroundings, causing a shrinkage to the landscape. Some recent reactions against whiteness by locals and architects, where the legislation allowed for it, resulted in the return of uncoated stone walls or light ochre.

Customising the Myth: the Holiday House

During the late 20th century the emergence and consolidation of the tourism market in the Aegean Archipelago created services that catered for the sale and consumption of nature—primarily the sun and the sea—as well as the 'picturesque' landscape and 'housescape'. Their representations were constructed and controlled by the media, the state (through the NGTO and the Ministry of Tourism), international travel agencies and companies in the form of advertisement, souvenirs, food, folk art, and other cultural objects. Together, they constituted the image of the 'special' tourist experience. Applied in the microcosm of the Cyclades, marketing strategies categorized each island according to their target groups as 'exotic', 'wild', 'virgin', 'traditional' or 'cosmopolitan', and advertised the islands in general for their white picturesque houses, sunny beaches, and laid-back life. The tourist market could cater to all kinds of tastes, explorations, and extravagances but in order to appeal simultaneously to people with different tastes, their material expressions came in standardized formats. The standardization of the form of the Cycladic house was similarly a conventional adjustment of a local form, that responded to tourists' demand for authenticity.

Architecture is one of the boldest material expressions of the development of tourism as it is responsive to these myths, regulations, and expectations, and has a visible and lasting impact on the areas that are tourist destinations. It also facilitates the temporary increase of an area's population—even by ten times in one month—that is planned through national, international, public and private policies. An individual real estate market started growing in the Cyclades, alongside the local markets of house rentals and family businesses, and the tourist accommodations that were controlled by travel companies. Greek and international travelers, either originating from these islands or having fallen in love with them, wanted to buy land and build seasonal houses—occupied for only a few months each year. These houses were shaped by the owner's subjectivity, desires and needs in dialogue with the architect's vision, skill and personal style,and according to the local legislation on construction.

The gaze of the modern travelers was no longer fixed on the travel literature, ancient myths, or the Modernist representations but on selected bits and pieces of those, flooding in an ahistorical continuity, of which the most important component was the belief that travel was a vital element of a life worth living. Travelers needed a peaceful shelter where they could escape from the turbulent city life at home. Isolated from the rest of the world, their problems and their routines, travelers sought in the holiday house a safe yet unmediated contact with nature and an opportunity to see the stars in the clear skies, to swim, get vitamin D and be reminded that life can be simple and free of trouble. They wanted their body to experience otherness, difference, without being completely dislodged from its comfort zone.

The choice between commissioning the construction of a house to an architect and following the standards expressed the owners' status, personal taste and milieu. Some architects who had for years studied the local and traditional Cycladic elements and functions, tried to establish a new dialogue with the already existing natural and artificial environments. Their task was to design a house that would be resided temporarily, equipped with or deprived of the miracles of technology and modern life comforts according to its owner's will. Their professional challenge was to design aesthetic forms that would treat the space in interesting and functional ways, and would sit in a balanced co-existence with the natural and cultural surroundings. Since their first appearance in the Cyclades in the late 1960s, construction of such houses—some of which are unique in their form and the dialogue they generate with the locality—has been ongoing.

One such example is the holiday house that Iannis Xenakis designed for his friend, the French composer François-Bernard Mâche, close to Lefkes village in Amorgos. The house was designed in 1966, but not completed until 1977 due to the architect's absence and difficulties arising from the house's location and the lack of infrastructure.

Mâche's villa was designed as if in correspondence with the local architecture. It innovatively dealt with functionality, offering comfort in terms of space management but also placing a limit on this comfort through the almost ascetic simplicity of the forms and the built-in furnishings. Community and isolation were strictly organized in the interior through autonomous spaces with distinct uses according to the owner's desire. The exterior was designed perimetrically, offering different sitting options according to the movement of the sun.

Contact with the surroundings—nature and sound—was both restricted and unhindered by the particular openings-fissures that allow the house to be simultaneously exposed and protected from the strong summer light. The uniquely shaped windows impose their strongly suggested form on the surrounding landscape when looked through, constantly reminding the spirit of Modernism and the signature of the artist. Inspired by the details he had invented while being involved in Le Corbusier's project for *La Tourette* and similar plans that shared the same architectural language, (such as the bergerie of René Schneider in Corsica and the drawings for the unrealized house for Karen and Roger Reynolds at Borrego Springs), Xenakis' design was not site-specific or singular.

Vernacular Cycladic architecture was shaped to meet the direct needs of its residents; its poorly-copied versions and adaptations meant to meet the needs of the massive sun and sea tourism; while more recent, authored designs of houses in the Cycladic region sought to converse with it. Villa Mâche stands aesthetically and spatially in a remote and probably inadvertent correspondence with the idioms of the anonymous and unscientific Cycladic architecture.

Dimitra Kondylatou is a visual artist living in Athens. Through moving-image, editing, writing, and hosting, she explores art's entanglements with tourism and everyday life.

Informal conversations on Amorgian architecture with Giannis Giannakos. June 2019.

Galani - Moutafi, Vasiliki. "Aegean: tourist destinations, intercultural encounters and socio-economic changes." In The Dispersed Urbanity of the Aegean Archipelago. Greek Ministry of Culture, 10th Venice Biennale of Architecture. Athens: Olkos, 2006, 257-79.

Giacumacatos, Andreas. Ιστορία της Ελληνικής αρχιτεκτονικής - 20ος αιώνας. Athens: Nefeli, 2009.

Hamilakis, Yannis. The Nation and Its Ruins: Antiquity, Archaeology and National Imagination in Greece. Oxford: Oxford University Press, 2007.

Kanach, Sharon. Music and Architecture by Iannis Xenakis. Hillsdale, NY: Pendragon Press, 2008.

Le Corbusier. Κείμενα για την Ελλάδα, φωτογραφίες και σχέδια. Athens: Agra, 2009.

Le Corbusier. The Decorative Art of Today. London: The Architectural Press, 1987.

MacCannell, Dean. The tourist: a new theory of the leisure class. California: University of California Press, 1999.

Nikolakakis, Michalis. Μοντέρνα Κίρκη –τουρισμός και ελληνική κοινωνία την περίοδο, 1950-1974. Athens: Alexandria, 2017.

Plantzos, Dimitris. Το πρόσφατο μέλλον: Η κλασική αρχαιότητα ως βιοπολιτικό εργαλείο [The recent future: Greek antiquity as a biopolitical apparatus]. Athens: Nefeli, 2016.

Stasinopoulos, Thanos. "Η λευκή ιλαρά - Εκτός σχεδίου δόμηση στο Αιγαίο." greekarchitects.gr, June 11, 2010.

Yalouri, Eleana. "The present past. Classical antiquity and modern Greece". In Y. Aesopos, (ed.) Tourism Landscapes: Remaking Greece. Athens: ΥΠΕΚΑ, 2014.

Woolf, Virginia. Ελλάδα και Μάνη μαζί! Edited by Aris Berlis. Translated by Maria Tsatsou. Athens: Ypsilon, 1996.

Iannis Xenakis, Selected
Projects from Critical Index
Sven Sterken

Fig. 30

La Tourette / Le Corbusier, 1956-61

Dominican Monastery with church, oratory, library, classrooms and cells. The Monastery of La Tourette is the first project where Xenakis is officially appointed 'project architect', working directly under Le Corbusier's supervision.

Fig. 31

Participation by Xenakis:
○ March 1954: first sketches; Xenakis' drawings develop around a sophisticated circulation system and the general functional organization of the plan.
○ November 1954: first complete series of plans and models on a scale of 1:50; the monks approve this proposal.
○ January – June 1955: Xenakis carries out corrections and modifications following the suggestions sent to him by the monks. He totally revises the project, with Le Corbusier, in March 1955. Xenakis

Fig. 30-34
La Tourette, Le Corbusier, 1961.

designs the monk's cells; the *machine guns* of light in the sacristy; the atrium and its tilted roof; the crypt with its *grand piano form* and its *light canons*, accommodating the monk's individual altars; the parlours, where the monks receive their private guests; the spiral interior staircase; the comb-like concrete pylons supporting the west part of the building; the 'combinatorial' glass panes overlooking the interior garden of the monastery, as well as the undulating glass panes on the west façade (for the different stages in their design between November 1954 and November 1956).

Fig. 32

In this project, Xenakis fully develops the aesthetic potentialities of reinforced concrete, as witnesses his design for the landing of the staircase on the roof terrace.

○ July 1955: The second set of plans is drawn by Talati and Tobito, under the supervision of Xenakis.

The latter takes care of the technical aspects: sanitary installation, heating, artificial lighting and evacuation of rainwater.

Fig. 33

O February – March 1956: Upon receipt, all estimates surpass the initial budget, leading to a conflict between Wogenscky and Xenakis on how to reduce the overall cost of the project. The project is scaled back during the summer, while construction works start in August of that same year. During autumn, the third series of plans are drawn by Talati, after a reduction of the overall dimensions of the project (suppression of one story).
O March 1957: Xenakis and Le Corbusier continue

to work on the church. The acoustical diamonds covering its North wall, designed by Xenakis, are eliminated for budgetary reasons, as well as the large belfry.

Fig. 34

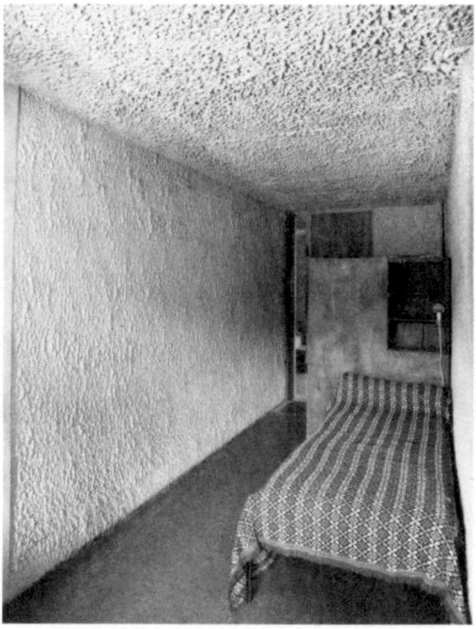

Vacation Home in Corsica, 1974-76

Renovation and addition to an existing shepherd's cabin. In the annexe, the kitchen, bathroom and toilet are integrated within an agglomerate of three organic volumes.

In this small-scale project (the annexe occupies barely 20 sq m or 215 sq ft), we recognize Xenakian 'neume' window configurations, realized by filling the negative of the openings in the casings with blocks of polystyrene, and removing them once the concrete has hardened. For the existing pavilion, Xenakis designed a new roof, detached from the walls by 12 cm (approx. 4.5 in). He also added a large cantilever in concrete (of 4.70 × 7.20 m or 15.5 × 23.5 ft), with a thickness varying between 6 and 14 cm (2.3 and 5.5 in). The structure was destroyed at the beginning of the 1980s.

Desert Home for Roger and Karen Reynolds, California (unrealized), 1984-92

This project for a house, in an isolated and infertile area, was conceived as an ensemble of pavilions, linked to one another. The house contains two studies/workshops, the main bedroom, a guest room, and a large two-story living room. The North and East façades are covered with undulating glass panes; the other façades feature the 'neume' theme. Between 1989 and 1992, Xenakis drew several versions of this project, with the desire to satisfy the commissioners' wishes. It was necessary both to adapt to the harsh local climatic conditions and stringent laws related to seismic protection and energy conservation. The investment required to construct it under these conditions proved to be prohibitive, and the project has not been realized to date.

Xenakis Vacation Home, Corsica, 1996

Vacation home conceived by Xenakis for his personal use. It is composed of two floors and has a terrace on the roof, accessible by an exterior staircase.

Xenakis' last architectural project. Each of the two floors was equipped with a bathroom and a kitchenette, to maintain a maximum of open space (axes 8 and 9.5 m or approx. 26 and 31 ft). The façades are covered almost entirely with undulating glass panes.

Fig. 35
Xenakis vacation home, Corsica.

Sven Sterken obtained a masters in architectural engineering and a doctoral thesis on the spatial and multimedia work of the composer Iannis Xenakis.

Originally published in Sharon Kanach, Music and Architecture by Iannis Xenakis. New York: Pendragon Press, 2008.

Image credits

Fig. 1
Iannis Xenakis

Fig. 2
Hülya Ertas

Fig. 4, 5
François-Bernard Mâche

Fig. 6, 8, 11–13, 17–20, 27
nibia pastrana santiago

Fig. 7, 9, 10, 14–16, 26
Vasilis Voskos

Fig. 21–24
Elina Loukou

Fig. 27
Christoph Hefti

Fig. 28
Alan Wainwright

Fig. 29
Anna Pipilis

Fig. 35
Sharon Kanach

Colophon

published in 2020 by
kyklàda.press

contributors
Hülya Ertas
Màkhi Xenakis
Sharon Kanach
David Bergé
Dimitra Kondylatou
Sven Sterken

copy editing
and proofreading
Sharon Kanach
Josie Proud
Julia Tulke

thanks to
Dušica Dražić
Elina Loukou
Peter Schmidt
Theodosia Stathi

design
Costas Kalogeropoulos
with Roland Brauchli
and David Bergé

distribution
Books People Places
and kyklàda.press

series direction
David Bergé

kyklàda.press team 2020
Juan Duque
Hülya Ertas
Dimitra Kondylatou
Nicolas Lakiotakis
Denis Maksimov

kyklàda.press
is an imprint of
PHOTOGRAPHIC
EXPANDED
PUBLISHING
ATHENS

Free Love Paid Love (2020)
Expressions of Affection in Mykonos

Nowhere in Cycladic culture has love been defined in a singular all-encompassing manner. Forces of attraction, affection, connection, and relation were ascribed in a plurality of ways. Through symposia in Delos, the tax haven of antiquity, 17th-century transactions of love involving pirates, slaves, and Mykonians; naturist communities reliving sexual freedom in the 1960-70s and 21st-century tourists quest in search of love, free or paid; this book gathers fragments of expressions of affection across Mykonos island. Mykonos has long defined itself as a self-ruling place far away from realities lived elsewhere.

The Architect is Absent (2020)
Approaching the Cycladic Holiday House

The white cubical house, the vernacular architecture in the Aegean Archipelago, knows no author. Its capacity to resist harsh climatic and topographic circumstances has been improved and adjusted through time and seems today close to perfection. The white-washed Cycladic House has become iconic to the image of Greece through the construction of national and tourism narratives. What happens when an architect steps into this process of anonymous transmission of skills? In 1966 music composer, architect, and engineer Iannis Xenakis articulated a response to this tradition and designed, from his base in Paris, a holiday house on the island of Amorgos while choosing to remain absent throughout the construction process.

Public Health in Crisis (2020)
Confined in the Aegean Archipelago

Epidemics and pandemics undermine societies and highlight the vulnerability of relations people have created to the land, other species, and each other. This book presents fragments of disease management in the Mediterranean from the 15th century onwards and in the Aegean Archipelago in the last two centuries. From religious to medical approaches to the Bubonic Plague, through the creation of lazarettos, to the famine in occupied Syros, to ghost ships drifting on the Mediterranean: citizens are forced to avoid citizens. Public health in crisis: confinement versus mobility, awakening memories of totalitarian regimes.

The Sleeping Hermaphrodite (2020)
Waking up from a Lethargic Confinement

What can a reclining marble sculpture, conceived through a myth in Greek antiquity, tell us today about the fluidity of our gender construction? What has been the role of aesthetic and historical canons in the construction of the female and male genders? Is 'the sleeping Hermaphrodite' really asleep? Or has she/he been induced to a long lethargic state, punished and confined by the history of gender normalization?

Architectures of Healing (2021)
Cure through Sleep, Touch, and Travel

Today, many feel fettered by insomnia, untouchability, and restrictions on movement. Looking for a more holistic approach to bodily and mental health, this book explores architectures and elementary forms of care and healing in different time periods: from the powers of sleep, touch, and travel in Asklepieia, the ancient healing temples for divine dream encounters alleviating the pain of the ailing pilgrim; to the attentiveness carried through the healing touch from the establishment of Byzantine hospitals till our times; to a pilgrimage center in modern-day Lesbos on a personal search for healing from the traumas of war and patriarchy; to the liberating and self-preserving powers of sleep as a healing response to past and current systems of oppression.

(Forced) Movement (2021)
Across the Aegean Archipelago

What would be of contemporary culture if we did not recognize the impact of migration in cultural and socio-economic crossings? This book explores human migration in different times, contexts, and geographies surrounding the Aegean Sea. Through an assemblage of voices, lived experiences, historical documents, urban and rural dislocations, this publication examines responses to mobility of the ones on the move, and of the ones living in the destinations the former are heading to. It speaks of the sacrifices one is forced to make en route and at its antipode; the implications of voluntary migration to a place, steered by investment in real estate.

KY
KLÀ
DA

Dry heat on your body. Bronze grasses and rocks, cactae, aloe vera. Concrete, asphalt, and marble, the Cycladic Landscape is both rural and urban: the Aegean Archipelago, south-east of Athens, extends into the city hills.

Through navigation, the Westernized sense of perspective has established a common horizon, simplifying islands as visual spots at the surface of the sea. Islands are not exotic entities isolated in the sea waters. Islands remain interconnected with the mainland and each other, from the top of the mountains to the hidden topographies of the sea-bed: a myriad of creatures and non-organic matter which lives in constant symbiosis with water; tectonic plates, fossil fuel pipes, and data cables.

kyklàda.press is a small imprint, producing a series of texts resonating with phenomena in the Aegean Archipelago. kyklàda.press is a not-for-profit book project driven by a transdisciplinary team directed by David Bergé, exploring critical and experimental positions in writing. With each volume in this series, we are slowly forming a catalogue of liquid forms of modernity: corporeal bodies—historical and actual, real, and imaginative.